DESERT

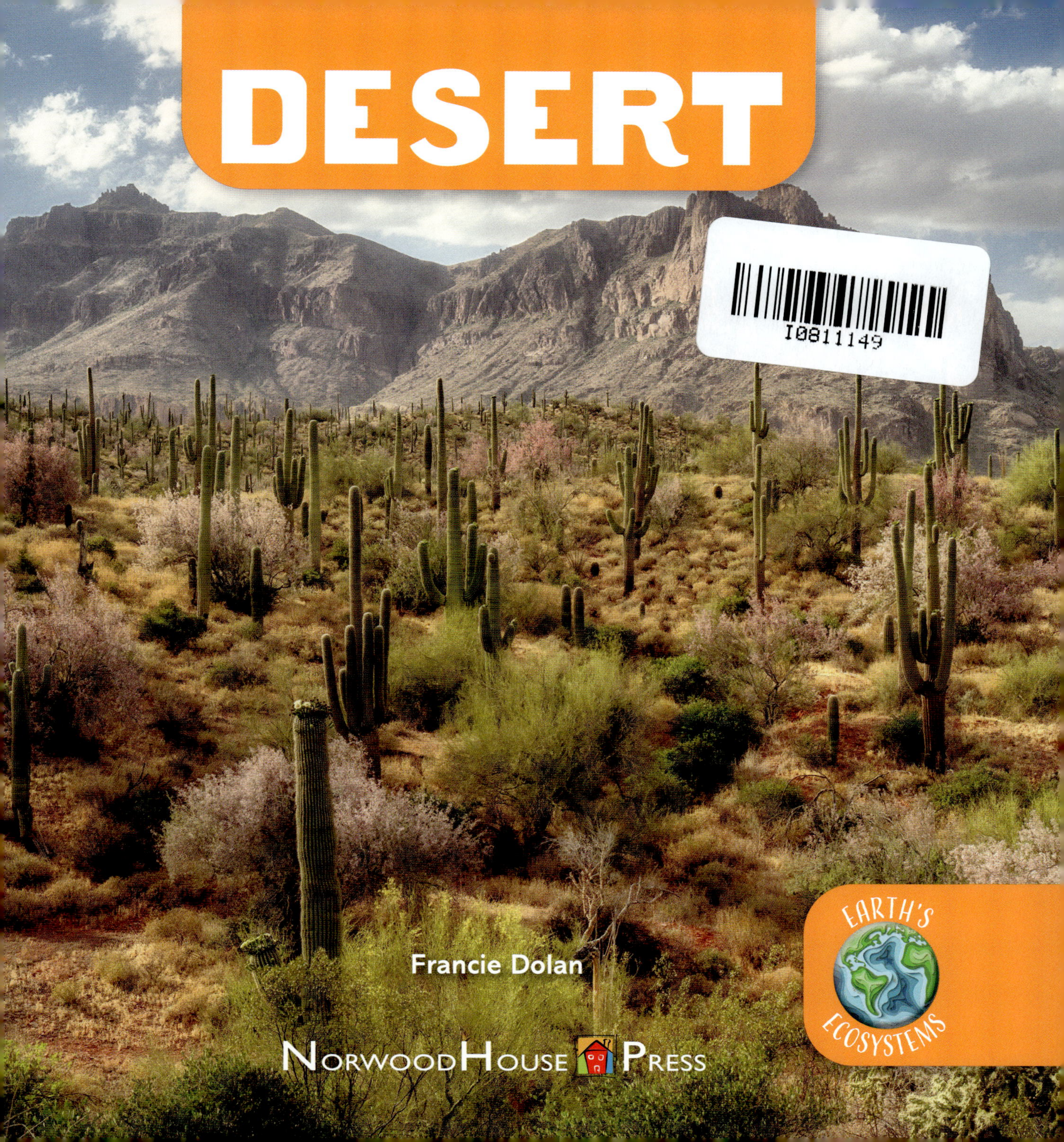

Francie Dolan

Earth's Ecosystems

Norwood House Press

Cataloging-in-Publication Data

Names: Dolan, Francie.
Title: Desert / Francie Dolan.
Description: Buffalo, NY : Norwood House Press, 2026. | Series: Earth's ecosystems | Includes glossary and index.
Identifiers: ISBN 9781978577015 (pbk.) | ISBN 9781978577022 (library bound) | ISBN 9781978577039 (ebook)
Subjects: LCSH: Desert ecology--Juvenile literature.
Classification: LCC QH541.5.D4 D65 2026 | DDC 577.54--dc23

Published in 2026 by
Norwood House Press
2544 Clinton Street
Buffalo, NY 14224

Designer: Rhea Magaro
Editor: Kim Thompson

Photo credits: Cover, p. 1 Brent Coulter, Kumer Oksa-na/Shutterstock.com; p. 3 casszee/Shutterstock.com; p. 5 Lubo Ivanko/Shutterstock.com; p. 6 LOUIS-MICHEL DESERT/Shutterstock.com; p. 7 Andrei Stepanov/Shutterstock.com; p. 9 LisLaz/Shutterstock.com; p. 10 B.L.Bowen Photography/Shutterstock.com; p. 11 Layne V. Naylor/Shutterstock.com; p. 12 idiz/Shutterstock.com; p. 13 Dominic Gentilcore PhD/Shutterstock.com; p. 14 RuslanKphoto/Shutterstock.com; p. 15 ALrumaih1/Shutterstock.com; p. 16 pic chik/Shutterstock.com; p. 17 bc_cornelia/Shutterstock.com; p. 18 Ingrid Curry/Shutterstock.com; p. 19 ranchorunner/Shutterstock.com; p. 19 Matt Knoth/Shutterstock.com; p. 20 BlueRingMedia/Shutterstock.com; p. 21 Brent Coulter/Shutterstock.com

Printed in the United States of America

CPSIA compliance information: Batch #CWNHP26: For further information contact Norwood House Press at 1-800-237-9932.

TABLE OF CONTENTS

The Desert Ecosystem 4
Desert Plants 8
Desert Animals 12
Desert Food Chains 18
Glossary 22
Thinking Questions 23
Index 24
About the Author 24

The Desert Ecosystem

Eco- means "home" or "environment." *System* means "a group of things that work together." Earth has many **ecosystems** that support life. Each is home to a network of living things that depend on each other.

One kind of ecosystem is a desert. Deserts are the driest places on the planet. They get less than 10 inches (25 centimeters) of rain each year.

There are deserts all over the world. Many are in hot places. The huge Sahara Desert in Africa is one example. Daytime temperatures there often reach 120 degrees Fahrenheit (50 degrees Celsius).

There are also deserts in cold places. **Polar** deserts are found in Antarctica and the Arctic. There, temperatures can drop to -20 degrees Fahrenheit (-29 degrees Celsius).

Desert Plants

Desert plants must survive with very little water. Special **adaptations** help them **conserve** moisture.

The saguaro cactus has a thick stem that stores water. Its shallow roots soak up rainwater quickly. Spines protect it from thirsty animals.

Yuccas provide food and shelter for many animals. These plants have long, sharp leaves that capture moisture from the air. Long roots reach water stored in **aquifers** deep underground.

Desert Animals

The adaptations of desert animals help them live in harsh conditions.

The kangaroo rat does not need to drink water. It gets all the moisture it needs from the seeds it eats. Large back feet help the rodent take big jumps across hot desert sand.

Camels have tough lips for munching on prickly **cacti**. Thick feet and eyelashes protect them from the hot sand and sun.

Camels can survive for more than a week without drinking water. Their humps do not store water. They are full of fat that provides an energy **reserve**.

A fennec fox's big ears move heat away from its body. This animal is **nocturnal**. During the hottest part of the day, it stays cool in an underground **burrow**.

Desert Food Chains

In the desert, living things eat other living things in food chains. A jackrabbit might eat the pods of a mesquite tree. A rattlesnake may eat the jackrabbit.

A red-tailed hawk might catch and eat the rattlesnake. After the hawk dies, a coyote may **scavenge** on its remains.

Many desert food chains together form a food web. It shows how all living things in a desert ecosystem depend on each other for survival.

DESERT FOOD WEB

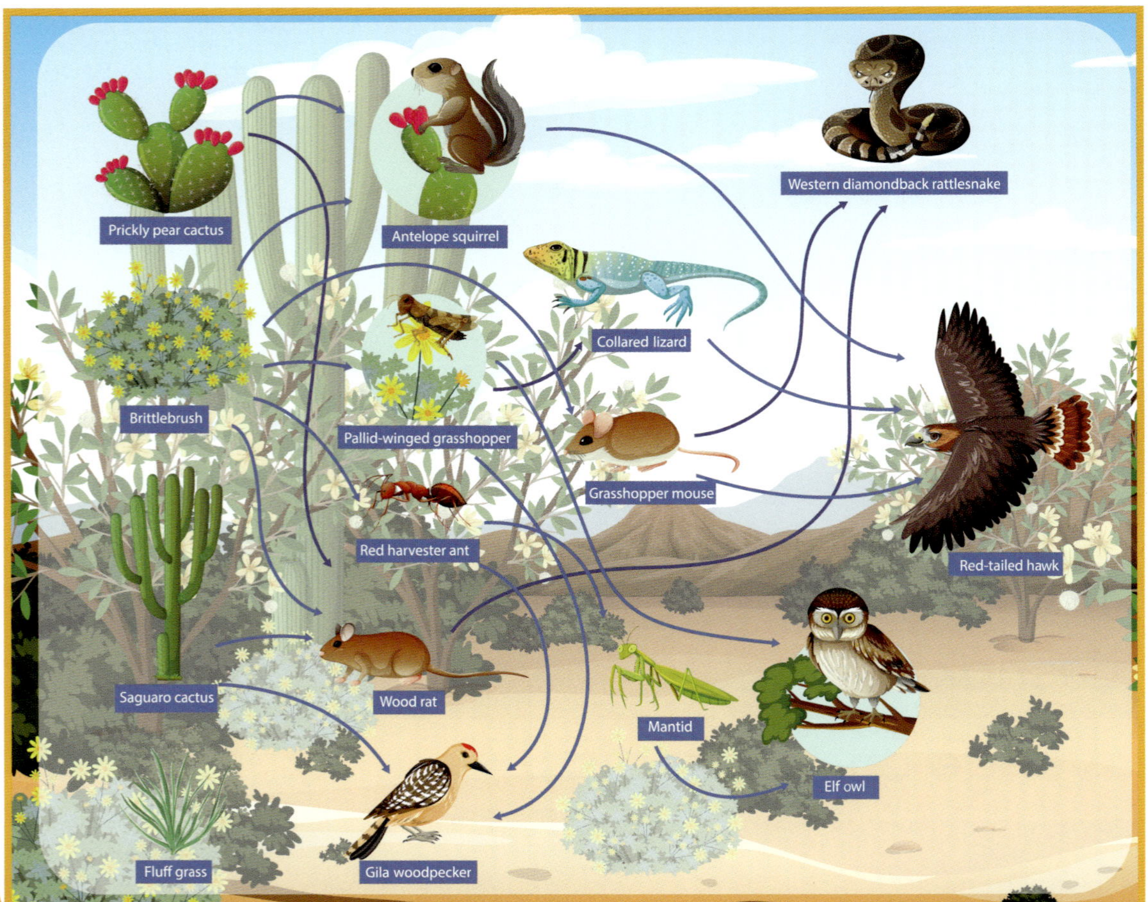

Glossary

adaptations (ad-ap-TAY-shuhns): physical or behavioral changes that help plants and animals survive in their environment

aquifers (AH-kwuh-fers): underground layers of rock and soil that hold water

burrow (BUR-oh): a hole or tunnel that animals dig in the ground to live in

cacti (KAK-tie): plural for *cactus*; more than one cactus, a desert plant with a thick stem and sharp spines

conserve (kuhn-SURV): to save or use less of something so it does not run out

ecosystems (EE-koh-sis-tuhms): natural communities where plants, animals, and their environment all work together

nocturnal (nahk-TUR-nuhl): active at night and asleep during the day

polar (POH-lur): having to do with the very cold areas near Earth's North Pole and South Pole

reserve (ri-ZURV): something saved or stored for later use

scavenge (SKAV-uhnj): to look for and eat food that is already dead

Thinking Questions

1. What is an ecosystem?
2. Where are deserts found on Earth?
3. Give an example of an adaptation that helps desert plants survive.
4. Give an example of an adaptation that helps desert animals survive.
5. What does a food chain show?

Index

camel 14, 15

fennec fox 16

kangaroo rat 13

polar 7

rain 5, 8

saguaro cactus 8, 20

Sahara Desert 6

sand 13, 14

sun 14

temperatures 6, 7

water 8, 10, 13, 15

yucca 10

About the Author

Francie Dolan is continually amazed by the natural world and how Earth's plants, animals, and natural resources are interconnected. From her home near Seattle, Washington, she loves to hike and explore forests, lakes, mountains, and the seashore. When she gets home, she likes to draw and write about what she sees on her adventures.